Little **Pebble**™

Staying Safe

Bike Safety

by Sarah L. Schuette

Consultant: Shonette Doggett, coalition coordinator
Safe Kids Greater East Metro/St. Croix Valley
St. Paul, Minnesota

PEBBLE
a capstone imprint

Little Pebble is published by Pebble
1710 Roe Crest Drive
North Mankato, Minnesota 56003
www.mycapstone.com

Library of Congress Cataloging-in-Publication Data
Names: Schuette, Sarah L., 1976– author.
Title: Bike safety / by Sarah L. Schuette.
Description: North Mankato, Minnesota : Pebble, 2020. | Series: Little pebble. Staying safe! | Includes bibliographical references and index. | Audience: Age 6–8. | Audience: K to Grade 3. Identifiers: LCCN 2018052291| ISBN 9781977108739 (hardcover) | ISBN 9781977110268 (pbk.) | ISBN 9781977108814 (ebook pdf) Subjects: LCSH: Cycling—Safety measures—Juvenile literature. Classification: LCC GV1055 .S35 2020 | DDC 796.6028/9—dc23
LC record available at https://lccn.loc.gov/2018052291

Editorial Credits

Erika L. Shores, editor; Heidi Thompson, designer; Morgan Walters, media researcher; Marcy Morin, scheduler; Tori Abraham, production specialist

Photo Credits

All photos by Capstone Studio/Karon Dubke

All internet sites appearing in back matter were available and accurate when this book was sent to press.

The author dedicates this book to her favorite biker, Gregory Monty Anderson.

Table of Contents

A Safe Ride

Let's go for a bike ride.

We can stay safe.

Before Riding

We put on helmets.

We make sure they fit.

Sam helps drivers see her.

She wears bright colors.

She rides during the day.

Riding Safe

We ride on the sidewalk.

We keep our heads up.

Mia follows traffic signals.

She stops at all stop signs.

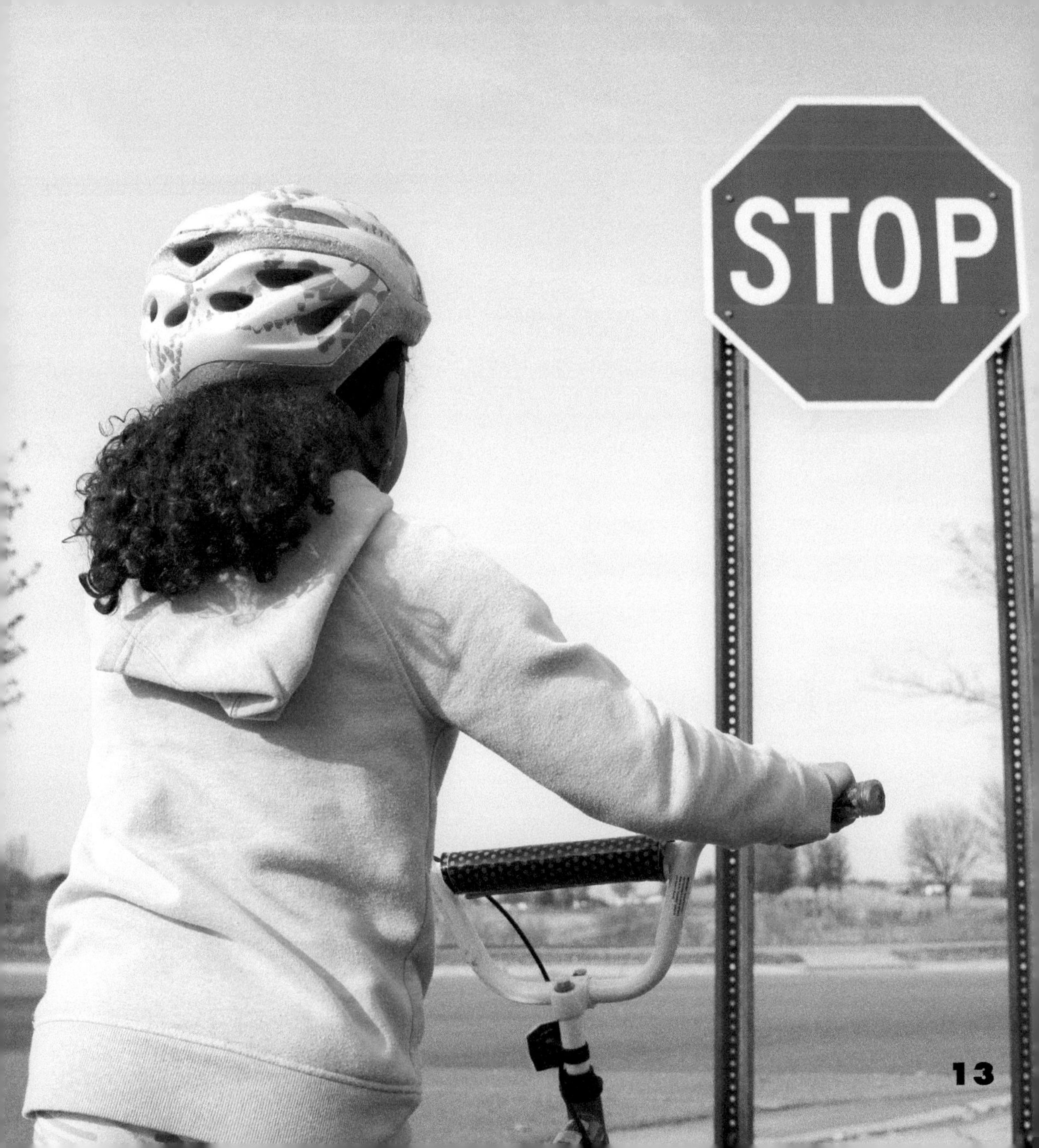
STOP

We look for cars.

We stop at corners.

Bo walks his bike

across the street.

Bri uses hand signals.
They tell others where
she is going.

A Fun Ride!

Safe biking is fun!

Glossary

helmet—a hard hat that protects the head

safe—free from harm

sidewalk—a hard path that gives people a safe place to walk or bike away from cars and other traffic

signal—a sign that stands for a word

traffic—having to do with cars, trucks, buses, and other vehicles that move on a road

Read More

Feuti, Norman. *Do You Like My Bike?* Hello Hedgehog! New York: Scholastic, 2019.

Heos, Bridget. *Be Safe on Your Bike.* Be Safe! Mankato, MN: Amicus, 2015.

Jennings, Rosemary. *Safe on Your Bike.* Safety Smarts. New York: PowerKids Press, 2017.

Internet Sites

Bike: Safe Kids Worldwide
www.safekids.org/bike

Bike Safety
kidshealth.org/en/kids/bike-safety.html

Super-cool stuff! Check out projects, games, and lots more at
www.capstonekids.com

Critical Thinking Questions

1. Why should you bike on a path or sidewalk?

2. How should you cross a street with your bike?

3. What kinds of clothing should you wear when biking?

Index